# DENIM
## AN AMERICAN STORY

### DAVID LITTLE

4880 Lower Valley Road Atlgen, PA 19310

# Dedication

For my Mom and Dad who put me in my first pair of jeans.

Copyright © 2007 by David Little
Library of Congress Control Number: 2007928034

    All rights reserved. No part of this work may be reproduced or used in any form or by any means—graphic, electronic, or mechanical, including photocopying or information storage and retrieval systems—without written permission from the publisher.
    The scanning, uploading and distribution of this book or any part thereof via the Internet or via any other means without the permission of the publisher is illegal and punishable by law. Please purchase only authorized editions and do not participate in or encourage the electronic piracy of copyrighted materials.
    "Schiffer," "Schiffer Publishing Ltd. & Design," and the "Design of pen and ink well" are registered trademarks of Schiffer Publishing Ltd.

Designed by John P. Cheek
Cover design by Bruce Waters
Type set in Humanist 521 BT

ISBN: 978-0-7643-2686-8

Printed in China

Published by Schiffer Publishing Ltd.
4880 Lower Valley Road
Atglen, PA 19310
Phone: (610) 593-1777; Fax: (610) 593-2002
E-mail: Info@schifferbooks.com

For the largest selection of fine reference books on this and related subjects, please visit our web site at **www.schifferbooks.com**
We are always looking for people to write books on new and related subjects. If you have an idea for a book please contact us at the above address.

This book may be purchased from the publisher.
Include $3.95 for shipping.
Please try your bookstore first.
You may write for a free catalog.

In Europe, Schiffer books are distributed by
Bushwood Books
6 Marksbury Ave.
Kew Gardens
Surrey TW9 4JF England
Phone: 44 (0) 20 8392-8585; Fax: 44 (0) 20 8392-9876
E-mail: info@bushwoodbooks.co.uk

# Contents

Introduction: Denim = Rugged = America  4

The ~~~~~~~~: Gold Dust and Denim  10

H.D. ~~~~~~~~~~~~~~~~ erica  29

Du~~~~~~~~~~~~~~~g  36

Ra~~~~~~~~~~~~~~ 2

D~~~~~~~~~~~~~d Cowboy

~~~~~~~~~rangler  66

~~~~~~~s "Bad Boy"

~~~~~ Fit  92

~~~~~anvas  98

~~~~~ Disco  102

~~~~d Acid Wash  104

~~~ Song and

~~ '90s Yen for Old

~~y and Ebay  143

# Introduction
*Denim = Rugged = America*

In a country that has always prided itself on its toughness, individuality, and youthful spirit, we share one common thread, woven through time and unchanged in popularity – durable cotton denim jeans.

For more than 140 years, the blue jean has lived to express what Americans have believed themselves to be; strong, unpretentious, unadorned, informal, comfortable, classless, hard-working, reliable, consistent, and improving with time. An Esquire magazine writer once called denim blue jeans "America's second skin."

If there is a universal uniform of individuality, it is the blue jean: An article of clothing, not a fashion item, that appeals to all ages, sizes, professions, occupations, political persuasions, and nationalities. Blue jean is a universal language word, understood in almost any country around the world, and manufactured and worn almost everywhere. What makes denim so appealing? There is a comfort in the continuity of blue jeans. They are something to count on in a rapidly and ever-changing world. The classic American blue jean remains virtually unchanged after more than a century. It is a rare thing in American culture to find anything loved for its sameness. In a youth-oriented, future-thinking society, there is precious little Americans can appreciate and count on to remain the same. And to actually get better with age and wear. We are attracted to newness, but with a fondness for "oldness."

We know we can always get another pair of blue jeans. And we know, that for the most part, they will be just like the pair we had before, and the pair before that, and on and on and on. Buying a new pair of blue jeans is almost reincarnation. We may never have another dog like the one we loved and lost, or another romance like the one that grew and died, but we can always get another pair of jeans.

Jeans are a common denominator, a great equalizer. Maybe we can't afford the houses, cars, and lifestyles of the rich and famous, but we can wear the same jeans rock stars and Hollywood celebrities wear. And we can wear them forever. Blue jeans are an expression of youth that we can wear for a lifetime. We don't ever grow out of jeans, we grow into them.

Blue jeans made of blue, indigo-dyed cotton are an American classic: One of the rare, truly American contributions made to the fashion history of the world. There is so little that is "pure American," but blue jeans are there, right along with Jazz, cowboys, and rock 'n' roll. However, like most things "truly American" they have their roots in another part of the world.

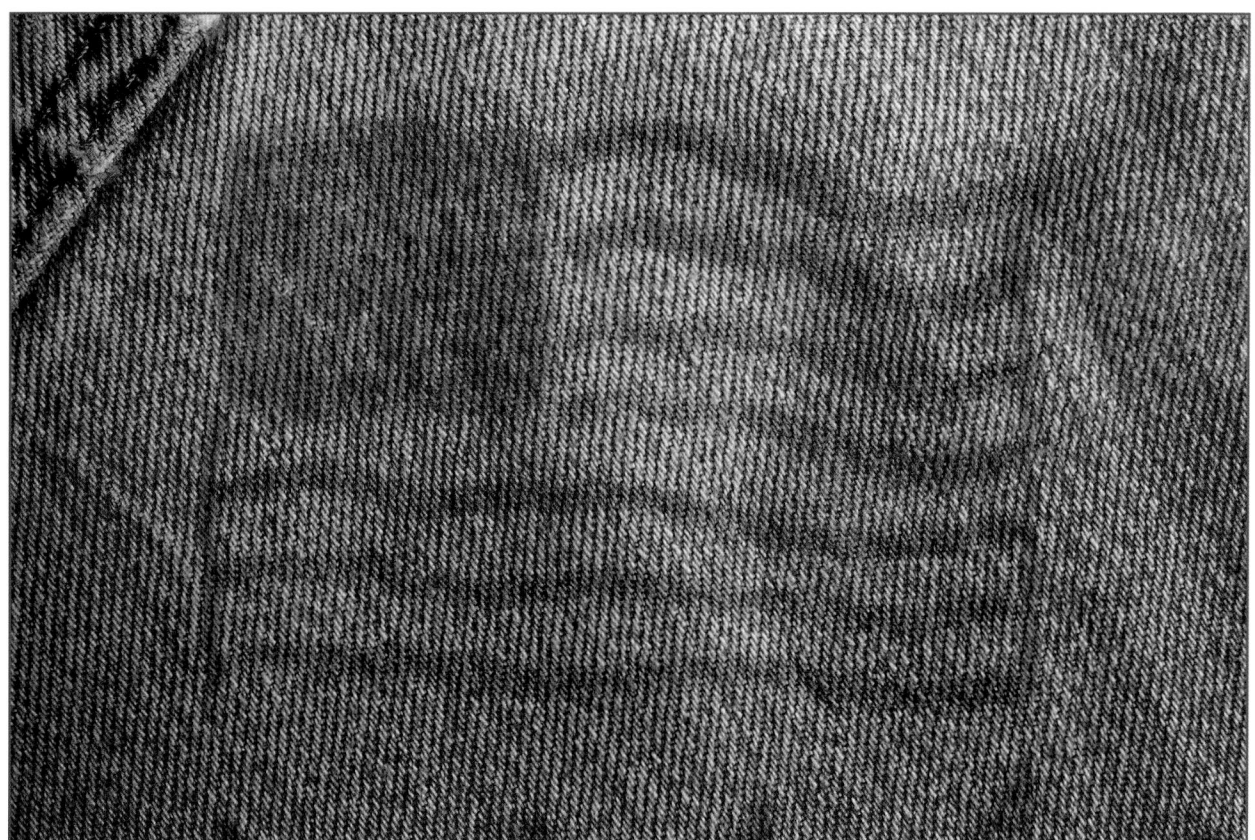

**Casually inspired, this patriotic addition adds that personal touch so treasured by denim owners.**

Americans of every size and age find blue jeans comfortable.

**Introduction 9**

A newly added tag indicates the enduring value of rugged denim jeans on the collector's market. The word "dead" indicates that this item had been banished to storage by a retailer who took it off the shelves some number of years ago and forgot about it.

An iconic denim image, Bruce Springsteen's Born in the U.S.A. album.

# The Beginnings
*Gold Dust and Denim*

The oldest, and still the best-selling, blue jean in the world is the Levi 501, born in 1853. Its inventor was Levi Strauss, (born Loeb Strauss in Bavaria in 1829) a 24-year-old who followed the wave of "Gold Fever," leaving the East Coast to peddle his family's dry goods to miners caught up in the gold-hunting frenzy of the 1849 California Gold Rush.

Strauss' fortune was not to be found in the gold, but in the brown heavy canvas, silks, broadcloth, needles, threads, and scissors he had brought with him on a clipper ship. During the three-month voyage, fellow travlers with time on their hands and some money in their pockets, bought up most of Strauss's supplies. He was left with a lot of heavy brown tent canvas, hoping to make tents for the hordes of homeless and hotel-less fortune hunters.

Most of the frenzied prospectors didn't care about tents. They were too busy digging and panning through the pomise-laden California dirt and would often fall asleep right on the ground next to their "diggings." They also didn't care about fashion. Most had arrived in the gold fields with the clothes on their backs – city clothes, which couldn't stand up to the rigors of hands and kneeds digging or panning and soon resembled rags. The knees and seats of their pants soon gave out.

History and legend often tell different tales, but legend has it that a ragged miner in a bar (where most good legends begin) asked, or better yet, bet young Levi Strauss that he couldn't make a pair of pants to stand up to the rigors of gold mining. Whether there really was a wager or not, Strauss won by coming up with a pair of sturdy, functional pants fashioned from the durable cotton fabric he had hoped to make into tents and tarps. The young traveling salesman had found his own El Dorado. His riches came out of the gold fields in the form of his waist-high overalls, as they were called, and became an instant hit with the forty-niners.

"The Birth of the Blues" came for Levi Strauss when his pants became so popular he couldn't keep himself in canvas. Strauss originally imported canvas by the boatload from overseas, but that took too much time and the demand was immediate. The solution was to switch to a more readily available fabric that was still tough, durable, and comfortable enough for his demanding clientele.

The fabric he switched to was denim, manufactured in a mill in New Hampshire, but originally loomed and worn in the south of France and called *serge de Nîmes*, for the French town of *Nîmes*. The word jeans supposedly has its roots in the French language, too. Sailors from the Italian port of Genoa, or *Genes* in French, were some of the first to wear the trousers made from this fabric. The weavers in seventeenth-century Nîmes were dyeing their strong, light fabric an indigo color. The dark blue tint was made from the fermented leaves of the Indigofera plant, indigenous to China and India. In 1897, German chemist Adolf von Baeyer created synthetic indigo dye through a completely natural process that had been used by the Blue Men of the Arabian desert, who wrapped themselves in indigo-dyed fabric to protect themselves from the desert sun and stinging wind storms.

By the 1860s, the Levi Strauss Company was well underway, with Levi's brothers, Jonas and Louis and his brother-in law, David, becoming full partners, with headquarters in San Francisco.

The new jeans were dark blue and stiff, but they were hard-wearing and softened with time. They weren't tailor-made, but a poor fit was often helped by a miner taking a soak

## The Beginnings 11

in a nearby horse trough in his new Levi's, as the pants were beginning to be called. There was one back pocket, and there were no belt loops, only suspender buttons and a waist-cinching buckle on the back. They were strictly utilitarian pants. The deep blue hid the grit, grease, and grime of a day's work, and they were strong.

They became even stronger when, in 1872, a Nevada tailor named Jacob Davis, approached Levi with a proposal to reinforce the pockets of his celebrated pants with copper rivets. Together, Davis and Levi patented these riveted pants (U.S. patent No. 139-121) and, with a few later modifications, the modern jean we wear today was born.

Levi's became known as "the two horse brand" of pants when, in a publicity stunt worthy of a modern-day marketing genius, Stauss reportedly hitched two draft horses to a pair of his denim pants and had them pull in opposite directions. The pants won.

The world's oldest internationally recognizable apparel trademark, the double orange stitching pattern on the back pockets, was added in 1873. The first non-functional aspect of the pants, it was just for decoration or, as some say, a tribute to the American spirit. It is said to symbolize the wings of an American eagle in flight.

The 501, a lot number assigned to the jeans in the 1890s, became such a success that Levi Strauss and Company could not keep up with the demand. Levi Strauss and his brothers were very rich men, with Levi's jeans at the core of this growing fortune. However, Levi himself didn't care for the word "jeans," and the celebrated pants were called "waist high overalls" by the company until Levi's death.

Levi Strauss lived to see his fabled pants gain a fourth pocket (for watch and coins in 1890 and a fifth pocket, (a second one in back) was added after Levi died in 1902. Suspender buttons gave way to belt loops in 1922 and the small red tab on the back pocket appeared in 1936. It simply said "Levi's."

Upon his death, Levi left more than a legacy of pants. In his will he would give away $1.6 million to charities, friends, and relatives, especially the children and grandchildren of his brothers and sisters. He had never married and once said that his business was "his greatest joy." He left his company and his $6 million estate in the hands of family, where it has been held almost unbroken throughout the past 90 years.

Levi's enjoyed a national reputation for many years. It wasn't until 1912 that another major manufacturer came on the blue jeans scene.

As Levi lay dying, his nurse inquired how he felt. He is said to have replied, "About as comfortable as I can under the circumstances." What he left behind is a legacy of comfort for the billions of people who have worn some close relative of that first pair of indigo-dyed, orange-stitched, riveted, button-flied, heavy-cotton, shrink-to-fit, denim garment known the world over as "LEVIS."

**When men began rushing off to seek their fortunes in the 1849 California Gold Rush, entrepreneur Levi Strauss followed in hopes of making the tents they'd need. Instead, he ended up providing the rugged wear required by the miners.**

## 12  The Beginnings

Levi's advertising boasts their role in taming the West.

Levi's double orange stitching pattern on the back pockets was added in 1873 and has become the world's oldest, internationally recognizable apparel trademark.

Levi's garment labels depict a famous publicity stunt pulled off by Strauss, in which two draft horses were challenged to draw apart a pair of his rugged dungarees – and failed in the test. Thereafter Levi's was known as the "two-horse brand."

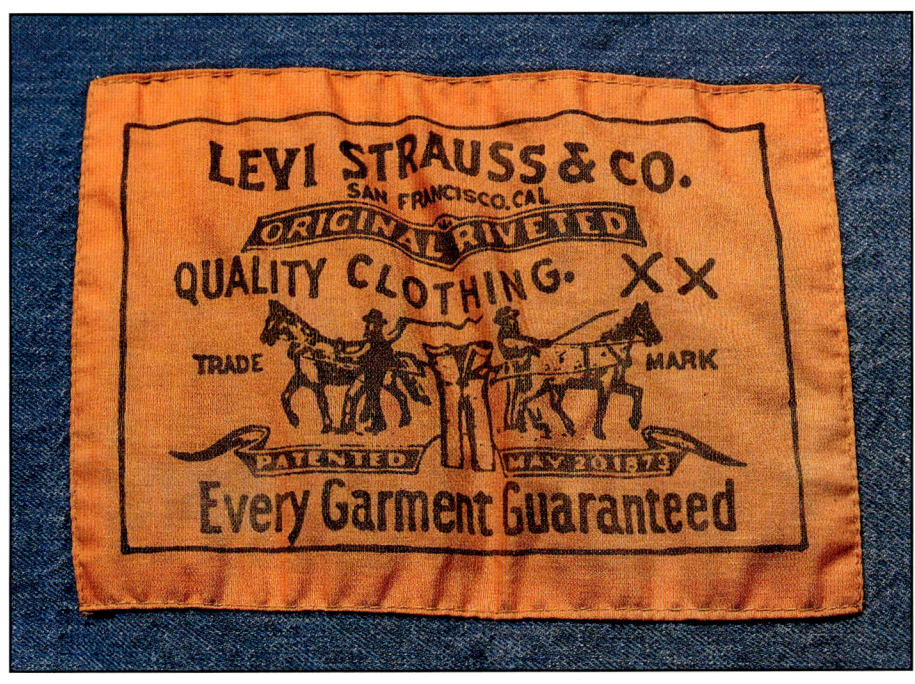

**14   The Beginnings**

A Nevada tailor named Jacob Davis, approached Levi in 1872 with a proposal to reinforce the pockets of his celebrated pants with copper rivets. They patented these riveted pants (U.S. patent No. 139-121).

Levi's earliest pants had no belt loops, only suspender buttons and a waist-cinching buckle on the back.

**The Beginnings** 15

**Detail shots reveal the waist-cinch and the reinforcing rivets that helped make these utilitarian garments so durable.**

16  The Beginnings

**Suspender buttons gave way to belt loops in 1922.**

**The Beginnings** 17

The original Levi Strauss pants had three pockets – only one in back. He lived to see a fourth pocket added in front for watch and coins in 1890. The second back pocket was added after Levi died in 1902.

# 18 The Beginnings

An exaggerated red tab on an advertising pair of 501s.

Artwork found on the plank floor of the Worn Out West vintage store in Hollywood.

# The Beginnings 21

# The Beginnings 23

A worn leather label in a blanket-lined jacket, a remnant of Depression-era hard times when down-and-out Americans invested in durable clothing to protect them against a harsh environment, both economically and environmentally.

**Reinforced, rugged double stitching and sturdy buttons live up to Levi Strauss's mission to provide durable work clothes.**

**A red tab and the patented wing stitching on the back pockets make these Levi's identifiable a hundred feet away.**

# The Beginnings 25

**Two buckle-back pants in near-mint condition.**

# 26 The Beginnings

Even with the brand name long since washed off the leather label, the association with Levi's is unmistakable. Leather labels were used from 1943-55.

"The rivet's still there," a tag tells us. Levi's patented reinforcements were concealed in the 1930s, some say to stop them from scratching saddles, others because teacher's complained that school chairs were being damaged.

**Girls were targeted, too, when jeans started their unisex revolution in the 1950s. Marilyn Monroe helped by donning denim and proving work clothes can be feminine.**

# H.D. Lee
*The Jeans That Built America*

In 1849, the same year young Levi Strauss was contemplating going to California, H. D. Lee was born in Vermont. Lee was a hard-working young man, and a shrewd investor, who eventually parlayed his earnings into a fortune that included oil companies and a wholesale grocery business. From his base in Salina, Kansas, Lee started several large companies that bore his name, but he was not yet known for what was to become the LEE brand of denim clothing. In 1911, Lee found he was having trouble keeping certain goods in stock, especially workwear items, including overalls and dungarees (made from heavy cotton twill and denim). Seeing a new business opportunity, Lee decided to build his own garment factory in Salina.

Lee's first claim to fame in the workwear clothing business would come a few years later when, according to legend, he suggested his firm develop a one-piece workwear garment. Legend says he was responding to a complaint from his chauffeur who was tired of dirtying his uniform working on his boss's automobile. (Lee's chauffeur inherited $5,000 after Lee's death.) Lee's workers sewed together a jacket and a pair of dungarees and the Lee Union-All was born. Lee envisioned this as the ideal outfit for farm and factory workers wanting to keep their everyday clothes clean while working.

The practicality of the new garment changed Lee's fortunes forever. The United States Army was so impressed by the Union-All that in 1917, Lee was contracted to produce as many as it could. His uniform became the official doughboy fatigue during World War I. By 1917, Lee had introduced more quality and comfort features in overalls, dungarees, and Union-Alls than all the competitors combined. That year Lee also pioneered the idea of nationally advertising work clothes and purchased ads in the *Saturday Evening Post*.

In 1924, the predecessor of what would become Lee Riders was introduced. These were pants made of heavy 13-ounce denim (Levi's were made of 10-ounce denim at that time) and were crafted especially for seamen and loggers. The heavy "cowboy pant" was to follow. By 1926, Lee had initiated a remarkable series of merchandising firsts including jeans with zippers, more comfortable styling, and tailored sizing.

Lee himself died of a heart attack in San Antonio, Texas in 1928, but like Levi Strauss, he left behind a pant that would bear his name long after his death, and a company that would live on to be one of the world's largest denim clothing manufacturers. Lee's motto "The Jeans That Built America" is a tribute to his tough, workingman's clothing and is a company slogan known throughout the land.

H. D. Lee hit on a million-dollar work garment industry when he had workers in his Kansas factory stitch together a heavy canvas jacket and a pair of dungarees, creating the Lee Union-All.

# H. D. Lee

By 1917, Lee had introduced more quality and comfort features in overalls, dungarees, and Union-Alls than all the competitors combined.

Lee pioneered the idea of nationally advertising work clothes, spreading the popularity of his brand name.

Lee adopted many of Levi's innovations, including the leather label. Their "brand" name was designed to look like a cow brand, to heighten their association with western wear. The "M.R." was added to the logo in the late 1960s.

A vintage Lee label.

**Lee also reinforced its pockets with rivets, like Levi's.**

A copper Lee button, the so-called "cowboy donut" button.

"Lee Riders" became a name brand in a bid for cowboy loyalty.

The addition of a new, popular innovation – the zipper fly – advertised among other features on a pocket tag.

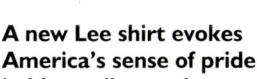

A waist tag for Lee.

A new Lee shirt evokes America's sense of pride in blue-collar work.

# Dust Bowl Denim
## How Depressing

Out of the ashes of failure, success is often born. The stock market crash of 1929 and the resulting world-wide economic crisis had much to do with the growing success of denim work clothes.

The Depression hit everyone, but its most visible victim was the manual worker. The railroad men, the farmers, the factory workers, carpenters, the working class men had all by now adopted the bib overall, dungaree, and denim jean as their uniform. America witnessed down-and-out farmers and factory workers, dressed in their working blues, splashed across the pages of magazines like *LIFE* and *LOOK* and *The Saturday Evening Post*. Whole families wearing denim, and not much else, were photographed as the stoic foot soldiers in this war on poverty. The enduring spirit, tenacity, and strength of these people was mirrored in the simple strength and dignity of denim.

To clothe this army of workers and masses of homeless "hoboes" who welcomed some honest work and a hand up, a multitude of manufacturers was born. New brands joined Lee and Levi during the Depression including Blue Bell, Big Smith, Big Ben, Big Bridge, Buckhide, Carhart, Union Made, Pay Day, Tuff Nut, and Hercules. Along with their thriving competitors, Lee and Levi's saw sales grow. Out of necessity, denim may have been the fashion, but it wasn't fashionable. It was not status wear, or "fun," or stylish. But the Great Depression, for the first time, gave denim an identity. It would be forever linked with tenacity, simple strength, quiet dignity, and power. It would clothe the human spirit during those terrible times and emerge as the look of a new American hero.

The days of America's "New Deal" further defined denim. Thousands of workers joined National Recovery Act programs and wore the red eagle of the NRA on the label of their overalls and work clothes. Denim jackets were lined with canteen or blanket material to protect workers as they struggled against the cold.

During this time, radio and national magazines exposed Americans to the music and images of different lifestyles around the continent. Railroad men, cowboys, country singers, and "hillbillies" became national heroes. Americans wanted to be, and to dress like, those heroes. During the late 1930s, the "Railroad Look" was promoted by Lee, which adopted the slogan: "Lee, the jeans that built America." Lee named itself the "Number One maker of railroad worker's clothes," and its advertising echoed that claim. They also claimed their work clothes were guaranteed against any defects and promised to exchange any item found unworthy of the Lee name. Lee used this link with the railroads and its "Union Made" label until 1955 in much of its advertising.

There was a solidarity among most Americans that had never existed before, a sense of belonging, and of suffering and enduring together. These hardships helped bring about unions. Denim work clothes served as the union uniform, representing the working class.

**During the great depression, Americans came to associate images of workers with denim dungarees and overalls.**

# Dust Bowl Denim 39

A dime was hard to come by during the Depression, and clothes had to last a long time.

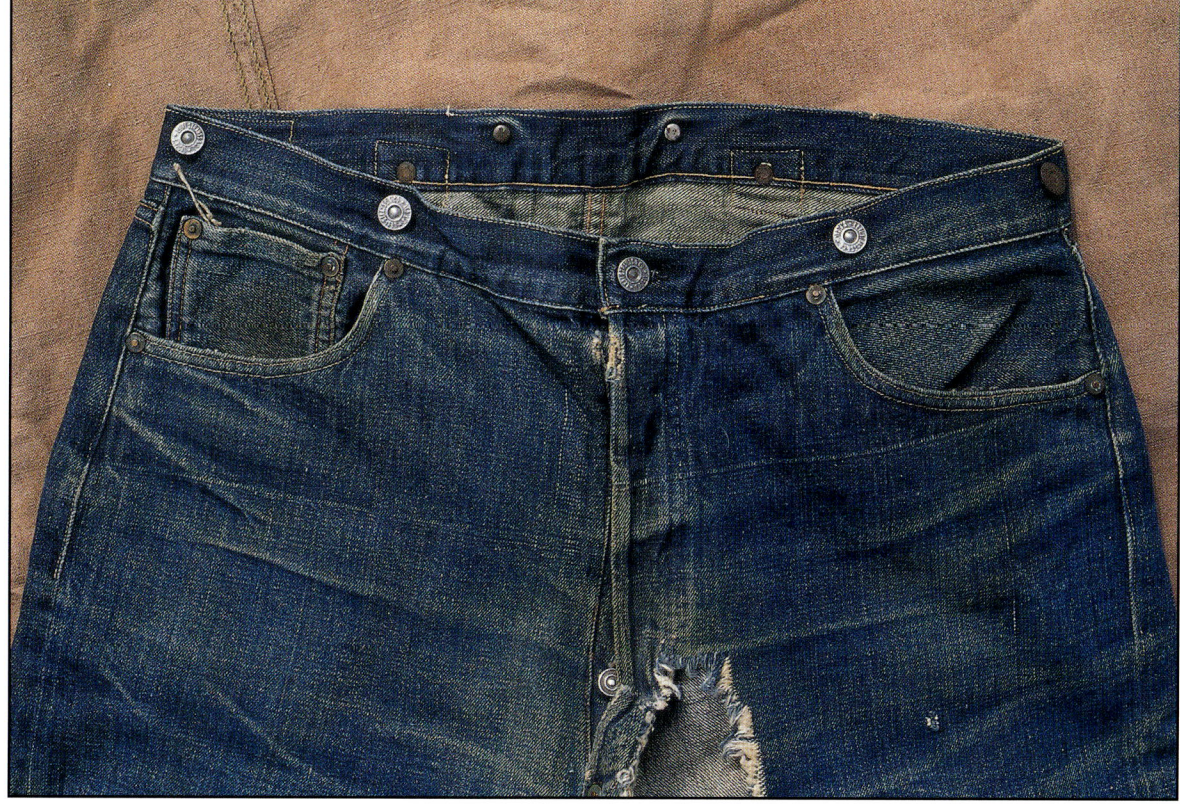

A worn pair of work pants, featuring the suspender buttons that pre-date the popularity of belts.

Many new brands were introduced during the Depression including Blue Bell, Big Smith, Big Ben, Big Bridge, Buckhide, Carhart, Union Made, Pay Day, Tuff Nut, and Hercule. Levi's and Lee also saw sales grow. The Union Made label is an early Lee tag. Above, Boss uses elephants in a one-upmanship move against Levi's "two-horse brand."

# Dust Bowl Denim 41

Boss brand top button.

Union-made becomes an important byword for worker-friendly wear.

# Railroad Style
*Blue Bell is Born*

The ancestor of today's Wrangler Company, the Blue Bell Overall Company, merged with the Big Ben Manufacturing Company in 1926, and emerged from the Depression a major manufacturer of denim work clothing. The Blue Bell Overall Company changed its name in 1936 to Blue Bell-Globe Manufacturing Company when it bought out Globe Superior Corporation. At that time, those two companies were the two largest in the world. Seven years later the name changed again to a simple Blue Bell, Inc. That company would eventually become the manufacturer of Wrangler brand denim jeans.

Early on, the Blue Bell brand stood out for its quality denim railroad wear: Clothing that was tough enough to last so that it eventually became one of the first denim collectibles. Before the Europeans and Japanese developed a taste for the old denim of these American railroad heroes, railroad buffs and collectors in this country were seeking out denim clothes worn by engineers and brakemen during the glory days of railroading in America. Copper, blued steel, and brass buttons with embossed names like Red Star, Big Ben, Ox Hide, Big Mac and, of course, Blue Bell, adorned the well-worn, faded denims of these railroad workers and were a magnet for railroad collectors wanting a precious piece of America's past.

**Lee toots its own horn as a manufacturer of railroad wear.**

Dust Bowl Denim    43

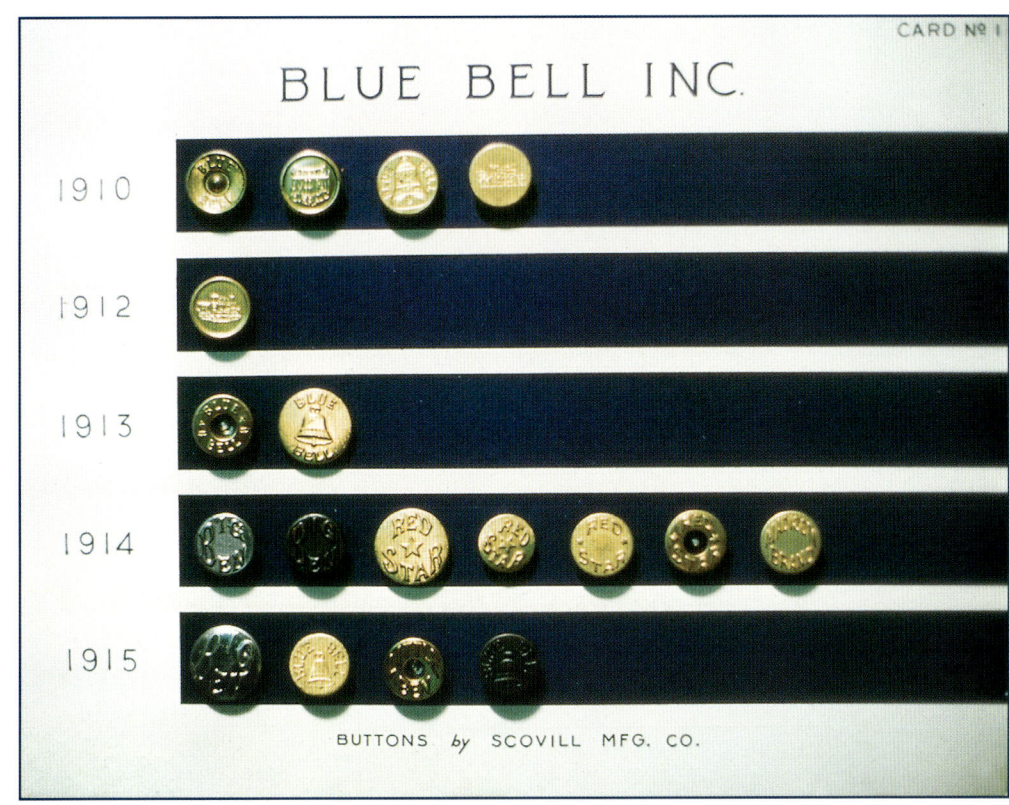

A button collection documents the early years of Blue Bell, ancestor of today's Wrangler company.

# Dust Bowl Denim 45

**Big Smith work clothes are among many collectible work clothing brands.**

**46 Dust Bowl Denim**

**Labeled garment in pristine condition.**

**Railroad wear was the first collectible denim.**

OshKosh launched its success on the railroad wear market, and has since gone on to create a line of children's wear.

Work wear has cycled in and out of popularity, it's most recent re-emergences on the fashion scene having little to do with the clothing ability to withstand rigorous work.

**Even children were outfitted in dungarees designed for durability.**

# Denim and Dudes
*The Country and Cowboy Look*

As the country was recovering from The Depression in the late 1930s, Americans sought new heroes. Radios, magazines, and Saturday matinee screens created a new icon for Americans to idolize. And that new hero was already wearing jeans: The American Cowboy. On the radio, Western Swing music replaced the hillbilly sound of farmers with fiddles, bandannas, and bib overalls. Now boots, big hats, and stitched shirts adorned the screen idols, whose blue jeans were rolled-up to show off colorful inlaid and carved leather cowboy boot tops.

America went crazy for heroes on horseback and singing cowboys like Gene Autry and Roy Rogers.

Lee, Levi Strauss, and a few other brands had already begun to align themselves with the western image and the cowboy. Lee Riders were created by Lee in 1924 especially for cowboys and the seam rivets of earlier pants disappeared in favor of durable, double-strength stitched seams. (Rivets and saddles didn't mix comfortably for cowboys as the leather got scratched.) A "hair-on-hide" leather label on Lee Rider cowboy pants appealed to the roping crowd. And, in 1936, Lee became the official sponsor of the rodeo circuit, much like today's Wrangler sponsors Professional Cowboys Rodeo Association (PRCA) rodeos. Everyone knows cowboys are loyal.

Much of Levis' advertising also catered to this working cowboy market. But it would be America's new-found prosperity and its love affair with the West and travel that would bring about the greatest growth in this market. Easterners with enough money to vacation were frequently "heading West" and returning with souvenir cowboy outfits. Guest "Dude Ranches" in Wyoming, Montana, and Colorado, were featured in LIFE magazine, where travel articles and railroad promotions guaranteed city-slickers a real taste of the cowboy life.

Western Style was born. While rodeo and movie cowboys tended to be a bit "glitzy," the notion of the real working cowboys, laboring in remote solitude, helped drive denim's image as "real cowboy clothes." In the style of Buffalo Bill and his Wild West Shows of the late 1800s, showmen like Leo Cremer and his "tough cowboys in jeans" helped spread the West with on-the-road rodeos and cowboy shows.

In the late 1930s, kids packed toy six-guns slung low on the hips of their denim dungarees and scuff up their boots imitating the likes of Gene Autry, Hopalong Cassidy, Roy Rogers, and Tom Mix. Many of the Western superstars claimed to have been "real" cowboys before being hog-tied by Hollywood fame and becoming American kid's heroes and Saturday matinee idols.

Were it not for the war, American kids would never have hung up their guns. They might have worn those frayed denim cowboy pants forever. But their dads picked up arms, took off their weekend Western wear jeans, and rode off into a different sunset: A world at war. So denim manufacturers changed gears to meet the special demands of a war-time economy and civilian access was rationed.

For example, Blue Bell, makers of much of America's work clothing, made the switch from civilian to war production. Company records say more than 24 million garments were made by Blue Bell for the Armed Forces as Army, Navy, Air Force, and Marine requirements skyrocketed. Those garments included jungle suits, denim pants, coats, fatigue pants and jackets, trousers, shirts, and flying suits. Most war-time advertising was directed at patriotism and "doing our part," not at selling products.

Product loyalty was maintained by promoting the company's loyalty to the war efforts and America's fighting men. Like most Americans, they hoped the war would soon be over and those fighting men would be needing new pants.

**Denim and Dudes** 53

Roy Rogers and Gene Autry became national heroes. Soon everyone wanted to be a cowboy!

The cowboy emerged as a bigger-than-life hero for Americans. His uniform — blue jeans.

## Denim and Dudes 55

Levi's was quick to advertise its "waist-high" overalls as a leader in the craze for cowboy association.

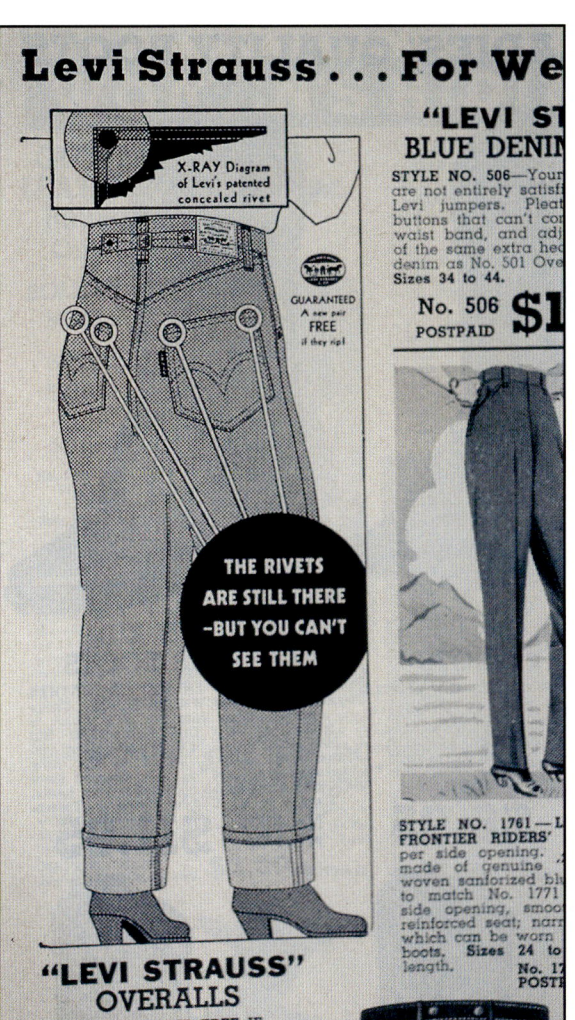

A lasso adds cowboy inclusion to Levi's original stake as miner's clothing.

Levi's famous rivets are hidden now, to protect a cowboy's beautiful leather saddle from scratches.

## 56   Denim and Dudes

**Cowboys outfitted in Levi's.**

# Denim and Dudes 57

Lee advertising aligns itself with cowboy gear.

**58    Denim and Dudes**

Lee jeans became known as "Lee Riders" as part of their Western image makeover.

Highly collectible Buddy Lee dolls were put in stores to advertise Lee's line of work wear.

Denim and Dudes 59

A Texas longhorn adorns the back pocket of vintage children's jeans.

Roy Rogers leant his name to denim wear for youngsters.

# 60  Denim and Dudes

World War II era advertising blotters produced by Levi's.

Denim and Dudes 61

**A pin-up girl adds kick to the cowgirl image.**

**64  Denim and Dudes**

Manufacturers were quick to target women for their novelty Western wear.

STYLE NO. 1771—LEVI'S ZIPPER RIDING JACKET AND RIDER OVERALLS FOR LADIES . . . Especially woven 9-ounce sanforized, smooth-back blue denim, made only as LEVI-STRAUSS can make them. This jacket is tailored with two set-in flap breast pockets, pleated front, free-swing back; zipper front. This jacket is made to match Style No. 1761 Levi Riders for women. Sizes 12 to 20.

No. 1771 POSTPAID  $2.85

LADIES' LEVI'S

NOTHING ELSE FITS LIKE **LEVI'S®** AMERICA'S FINEST OVERALL® SINCE 1850

**Denim and Dudes 65**

Levi's targets a his-and-hers market that grew up around popular vacations to dude ranches for city folk.

Holsters, metal studs, and equal parts leather and denim constitute the ultimate cowboy look for a young buckaroo.

# Cowboy Culture
## *The Rise of Wrangler*

When the war abroad was over, America's cowboy heroes returned to battle the bad guys via the medium of television, and we adored our fancy Western heroes on Saturday mornings.

Denim makers began a renewed attack on the civilian clothes market. The war had taught companies a lot about mass-production. The companies soon realized that, in the aftermath of the war and the rise in American prosperity and abundance, they needed to make the switch from work clothes to play clothes. Postwar America wanted to have fun.

One of the biggest markets was western wear. The popularity of Westerns on TV and the movies was at an all-time high, tourists from the East still went West for the Dude Ranch experience and would come home with their stiff, dark jeans, leather boots, and big hats. Diversification into western wear led to such changes as the giant company Blue Bell changing its moniker as "The World's Largest Producer of Work Clothes" to "The World's Largest Producer of Work and Play Clothes." This change spawned the birth of the national brand name "Wrangler" in 1947 with a brand of jeans made exclusively for cowboys.

Today, those same Wrangler jeans are the official jeans of the Professional Rodeo Cowboys Association and are often required wear during rodeo competitions. Rodeo is the one sport where the spectators can wear the exact same clothes as the athletes, and most do dress western for rodeos. In fact, the "W" design stitched into the two back pockets of Wrangler jeans supposedly stands for "Western Wear." By allying itself with rodeo stars, Wrangler became almost synonymous with western wear and its cowboy heroes.

**Opposing page:
Blue Bell began its name transformation with a brand targeted toward cowboys.**

**Early garment labels.**

Cowboy Culture 69

A 1950s advertisement makes the cowboy connection.

Wrangler uses the rodeo to market its clothes.

## 70 Cowboy Culture

A garment tag labeling Blue Bell's Wranglers the "real Western wear."

The "W" design stitched into the two back pockets of Wrangler jeans supposedly stands for "Western Wear."

**Cowboy Culture** 73

A 1950s studded denim shirt.

A studded belt and vintage Wranglers.

**Western accouterments against a backdrop of denim blue.**

Cowboy crossed with bad boy for a very sexy look

# Cowboy Culture 77

**Wranglers for her, Levi's for him.**

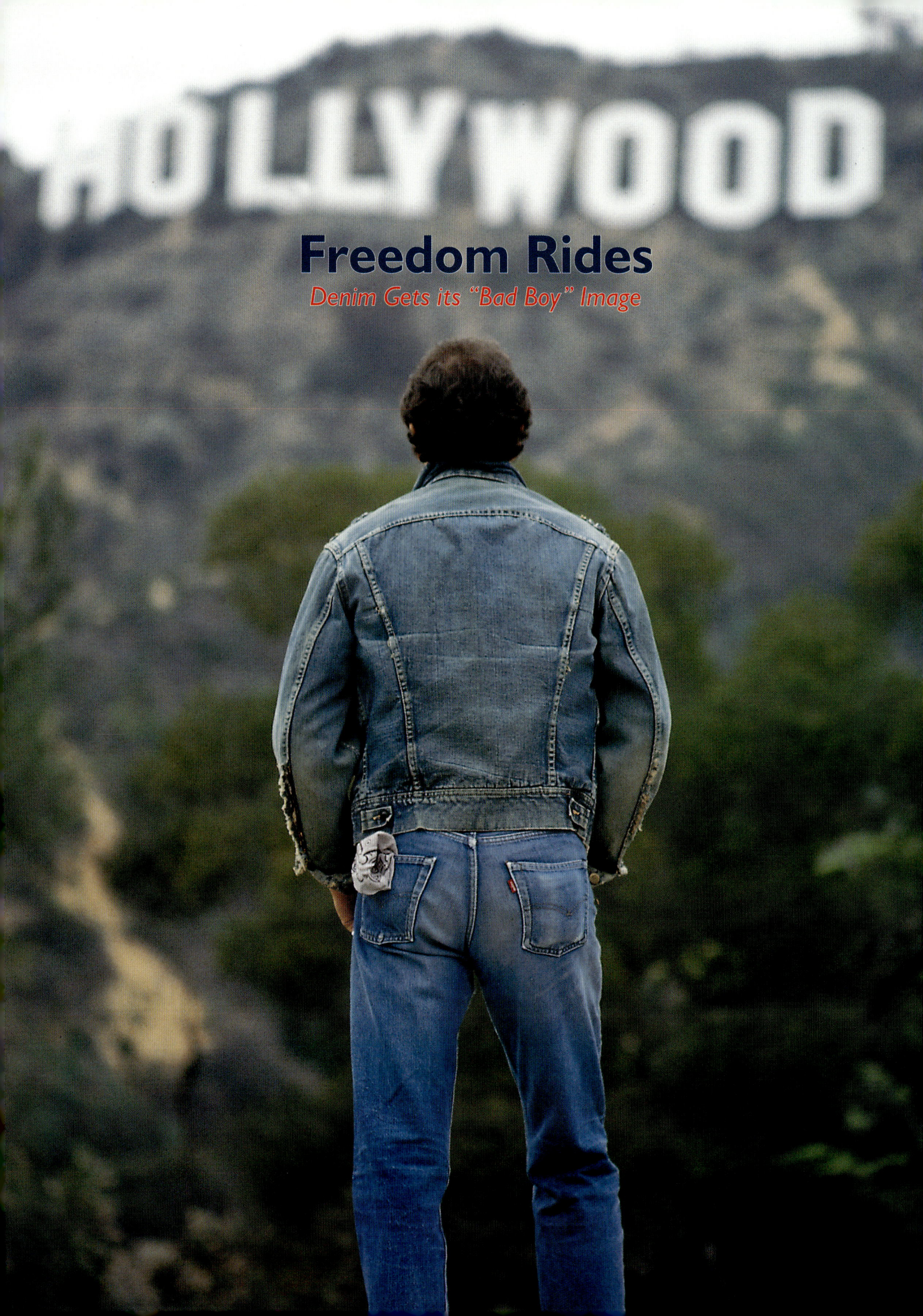

Post-war America would soon have a new hero, or in this case, an anti-hero, who wore blue jeans: The biker.

The thousands of service men who had been riding motorcycles in the service and in combat, came home with a love for motorcycles and the freedom they represented. The bikes most of them had ridden in the war, big Harley-Davidsons, weren't available to the public again until 1947. So ex-soldiers took to the streets on bikes they built from parts. Many of them radically changed the original design and overall appearance of their motorcycles. These were the first true "custom bikes," but not as we know them now. These bikes, with their stripped-down look, are known as "bobbers" or "choppers" for their bobbed fenders or cut-up and modified frames.

Motorcycle clubs began to spring up around the country. Soldiers returning from war often have a difficult time adjusting to normal civilian life after living a life on the edge. Some had grown accustomed to a free, unrestricted style of riding, and after the strict regimens and disciplines of being in the armed forces, they wanted to cut loose with their pent-up energy from the war and they wanted to have some fun. A few of these groups, most notably in California where many veterans re-relocated following the war, were still looking for trouble and were almost war-like in their aggression and customs.

Some riders went so far as to speed, to blast the roadside with the sound of unmuffled exhaust pipes, to weave in and out of traffic, and to "cut up" at rallies and race meets.

Unleashed on civilian roads, some of these disaffected veterans became known as "outlaw bikers." Unfortunately, the press and notoriety they were receiving attached itself to just about anyone who rode a motorcycle.

The image of motorcycles and those who rode them would forever change following perhaps the most notorious event in post-war motorcycle history. What made the rowdy antics of a bunch of beer-guzzling, bobber riding, "outlaw" motorcyclists in Hollister, California in 1947 so interesting and caused such great alarm across America was the fact that LIFE magazine photographers were there to capture it all. So, perhaps these "bikers" as they were beginning to be known, did act up for the cameras, perhaps even some of the pictures were staged, but somehow this "out of proportion" publicity became the basis for the Marlon Brando movie The Wild One.

Loosely based on the event in Hollister as depicted by the national media, The Wild One was released on July 4, 1953 and signaled the birth of the "biker cult." This Stanley Kramer movie became the blueprint for every other B Grade, outlaw-gang-wild-biker movie to be made, a genre that lasted for decades. Although Marlon Brando actually rode a Triumph in that movie, it was Harley-Davidson that became associated with the abhorrent behavior of motorcycle riders.

Marlon Brando and Lee Marvin gave national exposure to the "biker look," a look coveted and imitated by a generation of teenage rebels, "biker wannabees." You didn't have to ride a motorcycle, but to dress the part required a black leather motorcycle jacket, a T-shirt, black leather engineer boots with a buckled strap across the ankle, and of course, a pair of jeans. Almost exclusively these jeans were Levi button-fly 501 jeans. The essential element of the biker look called for the jeans to be rolled up at the cuff, well-worn, if not greasy, thumbs insolently hooked in the front pockets. A scowling, sideways sneer and long sideburns completed the look. The bad boy look was here to stay.

Elvis Presley, and James Dean help to bring this bad boy image to mainstream America. A whole new sound, Rock 'n' Roll, emerged as the soundtrack for a generation quickly shedding the styles and values of their parents. Tired of the drab sameness of a world in war uniforms, rebels and rockers slipped into tight denim jeans to proclaim their individuality and to flaunt their youth. Jeans became the uniform of the young. Millions of teenagers expressed their individuality and uniqueness by dressing almost identically, at least, as far as wearing denim jeans. The "uniform of non-conformity" had arrived.

Denim's new glory arose from its association with cowboys, strong, free riding, masculine loners who lived by their own rules. That image transferred easily to the "lone wolf" motorcycle riders of the Fifties.

Jeans, like Rock 'n' Roll, were subversive. When Elvis Presley swayed his hips suggestively in his jeans, denim became sexual. No adult, unless they were a farmer or a rancher, wore denim. It was too low class, too reminiscent of the Depression, and now, it was too vulgar and too young.

## Biker Wear

Bikers wear blue jeans. Or, not to be pegged as predictable, they might wear black jeans. If they aren't wearing leather, denim is the garment of choice for motorcycle enthusiasts, weekend riders, hard-core bikers and "one-percenters," the outlaw motorcycle gangs popularized, if not glorified, in dozens of grade B movies of the Sixties and Seventies. Bikers pride themselves on their individuality, but out of a sense of belonging, tradition, necessity, or practicality, a certain style of dress, a biker uniform of sorts, is worn by a majority of motorcycle club members. Try to find one of your buddies in Sturgis some summer during bike week. The joke goes: "I'll be the one in the black T-shirt, Levi's, and black leather jacket." That describes about 90 percent of the 250,000 bikers who converge on Sturgis, South Dakota once a year.

So the costume made famous by Marlon Brando in "The Wild One," that of rolled up cuffed Levi's denim jeans, a T-shirt, and black leather motorcycle jacket and boots, is still pretty much the costume of choice for bikers sixty years later.

There is a practical reason behind the way most bikers dress. Dark colors don't show grease and black leather protects against wind, weather. and "road rash" should a biker lay down his machine on the unforgiving hardness of the road. And the jeans? They are worn for the same reasons anyone wears them: they are comfortable, inexpensive, light, casual. and they still say "rebel," especially when worn with the rest of the biker outfit.

There are perhaps hundreds of different motorcycle clubs or "gangs" (as the press and police like to call them) in the United States and abroad, but there is really only one club that "enjoys" world-wide notoriety: The Hell's Angels. This club is considered the royalty among outlaw motorcycle gangs. And Levi's blue jeans and Harley-Davidson motorcycles have always represented brands of choice as noted in the Sixties hit "San Francisco" by Eric Burdon and the Animals who sang about "jeans of blue, Harley-Davidson too" when referring to the outlaw motorcycle gang.

In his 1967 book, *The Hell's Angels: The Strange and Terrible Saga of the Outlaw Motorcycle Gangs*, the late writer Hunter Thompson wrote about the sacred dress of the Hell's Angels. Thompson wrote that the Hell's Angels are a very organized group and very protective of their fellow members, their rules, their history and traditions. A great part of that ritual and tradition is the wardrobe.

Most motorcycle club members wear an embroidered patch of the name and "logo" of their club, called "colors." This is usually worn on the back of a Levi's denim jacket with the sleeves cut off.

But blue jeans aren't just for bad boys anymore. Today, denim has found general acceptance among all kinds of motorcyclists, from outlaw gang members to an old geezer riding his Gold Wing Honda motorcycle on the weekend. Even manufacturers have embraced that love of denim and manufacture denim garments especially for the motorcyclist. With armor protection and padding added, denim is even replacing leather as a fabric of choice in many motorcycle jackets and pants.

**Freedom Rides   81**

Biker's dirty denim and a wild attitude shocked our sense of propriety, and stirred excitement in the 1970s.

Images of impropriety, like the Hollister incident, focused on bikers' previously unimaginable behavior.

**Marlon Brando personified the outlaw biker persona in the movie The Wild One.**

James Dean, fast cars, and blue jeans became synonymous.

84　Freedom Rides

In 1966, a book by Hunter S. Thompson fed a growing fascination with biker culture, and a movie soon followed.

Below:
Harley-Davidson motorcycles became associated with biker culture.

# Freedom Rides 85

Japanese gangsters were tattooed from neck to wrist to symbolize their brotherhood. The tradition came home with veterans turned freedom riders.

Tattoos, first adopted by Western sailors as souvenirs from exotic travels, became a symbol of one's commitment to counterculture back home.

Blue jeans, black leather jacket, and the casual comfort of a T-shirt: bikers freed us all from the constraints of formal clothing.

Bikers and law enforcement seem bound in an endless opposition.

Women, too, expressed their freedom through biker attire.

Ripped, torn, and faded flew in the face of mainstream notions of "proper attire." Those willing to buck convention, however, taught us the comfort of jeans at the perfect phase of worn and personalized, a second skin perfect in every way.

## 90  Freedom Rides

Made for each other...

The "casual look "was born and jeans came to represent a new-found American ideal: leisure time. Elvis and James Dean wore the uniform like generals in a war against the old morality. *Rebel Without a Cause* became an icon for a new youthful culture and it taught us how to dress: T-shirts and jeans, Brando's signature wardrobe, bespoke a new set of values. Jeans were symbols of a restless youth intent on challenging the values of their parents. And they said "SEX."

Marilyn Monroe put on jeans and never looked like a farmer. Jeans now encased young sexual energy and fashion responded with jeans being worn lower on the hips and tighter. Just as the gold miners in the days of Levi Strauss had jumped into a horse trough to get their Levi's to fit a bit better, teenagers were now wearing stiff, deep dark blue Levi 501 shrink-to-fits into the family bathtub. "Guaranteed to shrink" became an advertising label that our parent's would never understand. Our jeans were guaranteed to shrink to fit us and to fade from that deep indigo into a color "faded out to the sky."

Jeans were worn as a second skin. We had to turn them inside out to get them off. Putting them on was a teen ritual and sometimes a group effort, as we wiggled and pulled dark denim an inch at a time, sucking in our waists and holding our breath to get that zipper closed or that last button buttoned. "Tight fittin' jeans" became more than a song, it was an erotic signal recognized the world over. *The Wild Ones* donned flesh tight jeans in revolt and defiance of the old sexual taboos. It was time to flaunt youth and sexuality. Jeans were sexier than no clothes at all: They seemed to say "good times ahead" to a whole generation.

The good times rock 'n' rolled throughout the Fifties for denim. Denim manufacturers responded to the new demand for denim with a variety of different products. Double-knees by Lee came out in 1957 as an answer to mom's complaints about their kids going through the knees of their jeans in a crawling hurry. Other manufacturers almost went broke promising a new replacement pair of jeans if your kids wore out the knees. It was almost instant reincarnation for dead or dying kid's jeans. Seeing they were about to lose the adult market, jeans makers came out with "dressy" jeans in whites and colors, with center creases and pleats, with narrower legs, with "new" sanforized fabrics. For the kids, they introduced "novelty jeans" embellished with "cute" paintings or armored with decorative studs and rhinestones. As jeans moved from function to fashion, whole families were once again wearing denim clothing.

Jeans became as American as Coca-Cola as dozens of new manufacturers jumped on the denim days of glory. And the world, partly recovered from a devastating decade of war, wanted the good life and the goods of America. A new overseas demand for denim jeans arose. In response, Lee opened their first International Division in 1959 and their first overseas plant in 1963. In 1964, Lee was awarded a presidential award for making an outstanding contribution to the export expansion of the United States. Imitators and designers all over Europe came out with their own brand of jeans. Somehow, though, they lacked denim credibility. The young people wanted the "real thing" and weren't settling for cheap copies or local brands. A very early black market in American denim, (most notably, Levi button-fly 501s) had begun as the world entered the turbulent decade of the Sixties.

## 94 Jeans Say "Sex"

**Pop art icon Andy Warhol created this album cover for the Rolling Stones featuring a working zipper on a printed pair of Levi's.**

Faded blues personify rock 'n' roll.

Bared sexuality, underlined by blue.

Sexy in its simplicity.

# Sixties Denim
## A Civil Rights Canvas

Denim became a canvas for messages of peace during the 1960s.

In the early 1960s, fashion adopted denim and began to mold it into something more socially acceptable. Softer, brushed, colored, permanent press, and lightweight denims were introduced to the market. A generation had thrown stiff, dark, dangerous denim at the faces of its elders and the elders gave it back to them sanforized and softened. All the fight had been taken out of it. James Dean was marketing his own brand of jeans. Even the President of the United States wore denim. It had become middle-class, softened up literally and figuratively, and was now as threatening as blue suede shoes.

Even Rock 'n' Roll, it seemed, had abandoned denim." The British Invasion" of rock groups was beginning. The Beatles didn't wear jeans. They weren't raw and tough like real American rockers, they were "cute." British groups wore suits, or psychedelic Edwardian-inspired clothes from Carnaby Street. But Carnaby Street was a fad. Denim was a style. An American classic. Most of us still wore them and felt more comfortable then we ever did in wide wale corduroys and striped, bell-bottomed trousers.

Jeans makers, like Lee, switched from keeping up with the demands of post-war prosperity, to staying on top "of the quickening rhythm of fashion change." The post-war baby boom had spawned an explosion in the number of teens who would spend billions on apparel, much of it on jeans and other casual attire. Polyester and permanent press fabrics had a dramatic impact on the jeans market, as America looked for an easier way and thirsted for more leisure time.

That "leisure time" was often spent in front of America's millions of TV sets. And for the first time ever, those TV sets were bringing images of war, death, destruction, poverty, world chaos, and the Cold War threat of nuclear annihilation into our neat little family rooms. Suddenly, almost spontaneously, a pacified youth began to act up.

The millions of children born after the war, the "baby-boomers," had become a force to be reckoned with, not only in the marketplace as consumers, but now in the political arena and the politics of this country. A generation which had grown up in the "good life" turned their backs on their own providers, rejecting them as shallow hypocrites. They also rejected their clothes. Young people didn't want pre-pressed and polyester, they wanted real and authentic, natural and functional. They wanted their own style, but they wanted to go back to America's "roots." Denim jeans and shirts were the perfect uniform for this disenfranchised army of teenagers and young people. They grew their hair long. Women began to wear pants, but were no longer seen as tomboys when they did. They hitchhiked and marched across the country, protesting war, nuclear arms, and aggression. They felt real and wanted real clothes. Denim became a canvas as "flower-power" took over as a rallying cry for these youths. They painted themselves and their clothes with flowers, peace signs, and slogans. Jeans became a badge of recognition again, uniting those who wore it in common causes and signaling allegiance to "brothers and sisters" fighting for civil rights and against the war and the "establishment."

Denim became as free and colorful as the idealistic "hippies" who wore it during those "summers of love" in the middle and late Sixties. It was a time to get loose, and loosen up the "uptight morals" of authority, of "The Establishment." Clothing became looser in reflection, even the jeans. The "tapered" and "pegged" skintight jeans of the late Fifties and early Sixties were out. Big, bright, colorful, flowered and paisley inserts were added when jean seams were torn open to make pants loose and wide at the bottom. "Bell Bottoms" were part of the new uniform, but not those mass-produced bell bottoms and other denim pretenders. It had to be real, and it had to be your own. Personalized by the addition of bells, paintings, fabric inserts, or fringe, denim became an art form and it became THE item of street fashion. It was actually "anti-fashion" as young people sought to revolutionize everything from their government, to their sexual and moral values, their music, food, and religion. It was a great time of change, though the old original Levi 501, unchanged in almost 100 years, was still the jean of choice for hippies, flower children, and revolutionaries.

Half-a-million peace and music-loving young people came to Woodstock wearing jeans, if they wore anything for very long in that summer of free love and "letting it all hang out." Inhibitions were something for squares and straights (they were the ones not wearing jeans). By 1969, denim enjoyed a new status as revolutionary wear. Coupled with cast-off army jackets, combat or hiking boots, jeans said something about you, your beliefs, your desires, your sexuality, and your politics. Jeans were the secret signal among the freedom fighters in the American streets. They explained status without becoming a status symbol. At least, not for the moment.

# 100 Sixties Denim

No institution was sacred during the cultural revolution of the '60s.

Personalized, handcrafted denim expression was highly prized during the 1960s, and the remnants are highly valued on the resale market.

# The Seventies
*Denim Does Disco*

We could just skip this chapter. For most of us, even those still wearing denim, the 1970s are an embarrassment. The revolutionary and radical Sixties give way to the shallow glitz and glamour of the Seventies. Rock disappeared. Disco was in. The sexual revolution gave birth to the self-revolution. Money, fame, and fortune were the new ideals and jeans mirrored them.

This was the era of the leisure suit, what jeans maker Lee called " A sporty interpretation of the business suit." Introduced by Lee in 1972, it was wildly successful and popular with adults who, according to Lee, "began to share in the style revolution previously dominated by the younger generation."

The new look was characterized by big collars, huge bell-bottoms, wild colors not found in nature, slimy, slick fabrics. Even Elvis shed his jeans for his own interpretation of the leisure suit. We knew this is the beginning of the end for "The King" as he donned stretch-knit one-piece jumpsuits encrusted with thousands of rhinestones, sequins, and studs. Rockers became superstars and begin to look like circus performers, using glittery makeup and elaborate costumes.

Designer denim began to replace jeans. In the Sixties, denim united a generation and emphasized togetherness. In the Seventies denim became status wear. It led to separation. The denim you chose defined you. Different brands allied with different groups: rocker, rebel, redneck, Rotarian, ...

Fashion designers neutered denim, creating "unisex" jeans and trying to make so many statements that denim became too diluted. Where once jeans implied a certain attitude and way of living, they now mostly implied how much money their wearer would spend on a pair of jeans. Price seemed no object. In 1979, designer jeans were a billion dollar business. Designed mostly for women, jeans came with lace, paint, studs, embroidery, and a multitude of colors. No more making your own work of art to wear, or soaking in a tub with your new jeans. Mass production and instant gratification were key for jean wearers.

Overseas there was still a great appreciation for things American. Especially for American things from the Fifties. James Dean, Marilyn Monroe, Marlon Brando, Harley-Davidson motorcycles, old biker jackets, D.A. hairdos, Chevrolets, cowboys, the Marlboro

**Jeans in every imaginable color became popular during the 1970s.**

Man, re-runs of old American television programs and movies. Jeans, most notably Levi 501s, began to take on legendary status and a strong secondary market in used American blue jeans began to develop.

Flea markets in London, Paris, and Berlin were stacked high with cast-off well worn American Levi's. I watched a Levi 501 ad in a theater in London in 1971. It had cowboys and real jeans. A pair of Levi 501s on the black market in Russia could be worth hundreds of dollars. The rest of the world could still see what we in the States had lost track of: the simple, comfortable, denim jean that said "American classic." It seemed the only Americans wearing real jeans were cowboys, construction workers, and those too poor or unsophisticated to live in a condo, do coke, and really be "into" style. The Village People dressed like hard hats, cowpokes, and gay bikers and didn't wear designer jeans. Denim became one of the complex signals for gays before they came out of the closet.

Andy Warhol, pop-art master and one of the voices of the 1970s, put a zippered crotch shot of jeans on a Rolling Stone album cover in 1971. At that time, Mick Jagger, big lips of the Rolling Stones, was wearing skin-tight lycra jumpsuits.

The Levi Strauss Company itself had lost touch with its roots. Diversification into "fashion clothing" and their own retail stores had Levi turning its back on what product made it famous. There was talk of discontinuing the 501 jean – just talk, though. Levi's image had been built on working men's clothing, tough and durable and built to last. Fashion was too fleeting, too fickle, to change something that had worked for more than a hundred years.

Denim designers, and by now there were many as designer jeans began to take over the market, turned their backs on American classicism and any links with the Fifties. We needed to think of ourselves as more worldly and cosmopolitan. The Euro-American look began and jeans with French and Italian names (though made in Hong Kong) were being sold to us. To make them appear even more sophisticated and worldly, they were expensive. But even at a hundred dollars a pair, disco designer denim sold. It sold so well that advertising denim jeans would change forever. Sex, or the hint of sex, would sell us our jeans. Sex sold so well in fact, that for the first time in marketing history, it was no longer even necessary to show the product. Jeans ads had no jeans in them. We were being sold an idea, an emotion, a feeling, a promise of hot sex, not of warm denim.

In this country, for mainstream America, plain good old American jeans were dead, the death certificate signed in 1978 by Gloria Vanderbilt, Calvin Klein, Ralph Lauren, and dozens of other designers who pitched their jeans with a varying level of snob appeal. Seventies fern bars and discos had bouncers to check that patrons were wearing the "right kind" of jeans before they were allowed in. America began to wear denim to work, with tweed jackets, cashmere sweaters, and diamonds. Sevenites Style might best be defined as representative of an age of conspicuous consumption and a decadent decade of self-indulgence. The name of the maker of the jean became more important then the jean itself and designers were glorified as denim demigods.

It seemed the only Americans wearing real jeans were cowboys, construction workers, and those too poor or unsophisticated to live in a condo, do coke, and really be "into" style.

# The Eighties
*Slash, Rip, Tear, and Acid Wash*

The kiss of denim on the bare, fifteen-year-old butt of Brooke Shields welcomed jeans into the Eighties. In a sly reference to not wearing any underwear, Brooke told us "Nothing Comes Between Me and My Calvins." Calvin Klein sold millions of jeans. Women's groups pointed accusing fingers and claimed Calvin was peddling kiddie-porn instead of pants. Designer jeans had lived to see another decade. Levi Strauss cut back production on its 501s and "regular" jeans.

The gluttony, selfishness, indulgence, and overindulgence of the Seventies was dead. America woke up to the results of its excesses and there was an almost fanatical drive to clean up, slim down, and simplify our lives. Drugs and booze were out, health was in. Cheap instant gratification was out, saving the world was in. The young joined the ex-hippies in the Eighties version of the Revolution. It was time to tear down the old and rip out those greedy, money worshipping, self-indulgent days of the Seventies, starting with the jeans.

It might have begun with the Punk Movement in Europe. It may have been a display of disdain for anything flaunting wealth. Perhaps it was simply a fad, another wave in the ebb and flow of denim custom – somebody, somewhere, slashed their jeans. Maybe they just tore them a little bit. Then a little bit more. Then things got out of hand. People spilled bleach on their jeans – new jeans. They roughed them up. They ripped them. Quick-thinking American entrepreneurs, sensing a trend, blew holes in jeans with double-barreled shotguns and attached the spent shell as proof that they really had been shot. All in the name of fashion.

Americans, it seemed, were tired of the designer-inspired trendiness that had permeated almost all of fashion. It had become a cliché and the Eighties hated clichés. Designers hated losing money more, so they wised up and soon had Americans paying more money for ripped and torn, half-destroyed jeans than for perfectly good ones. Things were going full-circle in a hurry.

In the rush to become more laid-back, we were losing our patience. Despite our displeasure with the "instant gratification" of the past, we wanted the new good life and we wanted it right now.

Jean makers were happy to oblige. Just as in the Fifties when they gave us "time saving" permanent press, no-iron denim fabrics, now they would be happy to supply, for a price, something we used to have to wait for: Worn-out, or more correctly, worn-in jeans. Pioneered by Maritime Bachellerie and Francois Girbaud in 1965, the concept of selling "worn" jeans was not a new one. These French designers decided denim was too stiff and went about developing a process to soften and fade new denim. First, they would wash each pair four or five times, then scrape the fabric with sandpaper. This eventually spawned the stone-washing process whereby jeans were washed with pumice stones to soften the garment and give it a well-worn appearance. This pair would go on to father other "technological advances" in jeans including the Baggy Jean, the concept of "slouchy street chic" and, their company claims, the Torn and Destroyed Jean.

Jean sales peaked in 1981. Consumers didn't want, or need, another designer label of jeans. They wanted their old jeans back, but with a lot of life still in them if possible.

The problem with jeans was they had such a short "perfect" life. That wonderful time when your jeans were just the right softness and color of faded blue. What 1970s singer/songwriter Cat Stevens has called "faded out to the sky." This usually took a few years and dozens of trips through the washer and dryer. And just when they got "perfect" the fabric would usually have gotten so thin that holes would appear and jeans would go from being "perfect" to being worn out.

Manufacturers like Lee and Levi realized that customers became more attached to their jeans as they became more faded and worn and they began toying with washing their new jeans in chemicals, such as bleach and softeners, coining the term "acid-washed." This was a misnomer, they didn't actually use acids. But they did try about everything else. Lee said they ultimately experimented with hundreds of objects to prematurely age their jeans, including "shredded car tires, bottle caps, golf balls, rope, and wood." Nothing worked as well as pumice, a rock formed by volcanic action and used to soften hands and feet and eliminate calluses. Ironically, because of the battering jeans take during the process, much tougher and more (about 12 times more) expensive thread had to be used. So, "worn out" pants could be sold for more than regular jeans and manufacturers could barely keep up with demand.

Stone-washing and acid-bleaching weren't for denim purists, though. Original Levi 501s started selling again. Coke had learned the lesson when it brought out "new" Coke – people wanted "the real thing." You could always count on Levi 501s being the same. Very minor changes took place across the world of denim in the 1980s. New, faster and cheaper methods of putting together pants were being employed by manufacturers with less waste of material, time, and cost. In some cases, these changes were insignificant to the manufacturer, but to the jean purist, the connoisseur, any change mattered.

The red thread that ran down the inside of the leg seam on a pair of Levi 501s disappeared in 1985. The closing of a fabric mill that made denim for Levi was supposedly the reason for this change. No one would notice or care, would they? But just as small changes made in the 501 jean over the past 100 years could be traced and used as a kind of "carbon dating" to determine when a 501 was made, so would this minor change date the "older Levis. Though this minor change meant nothing to Levi or most 501 buyers at the store, it meant a lot of money to a growing breed of denim devotee: The Collector.

**Worn, faded, and patched used to represent age in a pair of pants. In the 1980s, we wanted old in a hurry.**

Rips provided an opportunity to show a little skin.

The Eighties 107

**Stone- and acid-wash treatments gave us faded from the first.**

As America's love affair with blue jeans and denim grew it claimed a prominent place in popular music. Girls in blue jeans, boys in black denim trousers and motorcycle boots were glorified in song at about the same time the popularity of denim was growing in America.

It was natural that blue jeans would appear in "the blues," for example the classic "House of the Rising Sun" a supposed traditional song made famous by Eric Burdon and the Animals who wailed about a mother who "sewed my new blue jeans," rhyming nicely with "down in New Orleans."

Jerry Leiber and Mike Stoller, who wrote a lot of songs for Elvis, wrote the song "Black Denim Trousers and Motorcycle Boots," copyrighted in 1955 by Quintet Music, Inc. That same year, this classic song, which immortalized a motorcycle bad guy was recorded and released by two different artists: The Cheers and Vaughn Monroe.

Crooner Eddie Fisher also released a song about the softer side of denim with his 1955 hit, "Dungaree Doll." Also in the mid-Fifties, Gene Vincent sang about his "blue jean baby" in the classic "Blue Jean Bop," a song covered by Beatle Paul McCartney decades later.

"Venus In Blue Jeans" appeared on the charts in 1962 as a hit for Jimmy Clanton. An English group named themselves "The Swinging Blue Jeans" and had a major hit with the song "Hippy Hippy Shake" in 1964. Another band in the Fifties was also enamored enough of blue jeans to find a namesake in blue denim when Bob B. Soxx and the Blue Jeans appeared on the early R&B scene

"I was feeling nearly faded as my jeans," sang Janis Joplin as well as songwriter Kris Kristofferson in "Me and Bobby McGee." Eric Clapton sang "I don't wanna fade away" in his classic "Bell Bottom Blues" from the Layla album. Texas rockers ZZ Top recorded "My Old Blue Jeans" as well as "Blue Jean Blues" in 1975. Neil Diamond in 1978 extolled the virtues of comfortable casual living and loving in his song "Forever in Blue Jeans."

From the Beatles to the Beach Boys to Bruce Springsteen, to Rickie Lee Jones and Carly Simon, songwriters used blue jeans to set a mood or character. Blue jeans appeared in songs and musical tastes from Rock to New Wave to Country.

Country artist Conway Twitty sang the sexual praises and allure of denim jeans in his hit "Tight Fittin' Jeans" in 1981 and also used the blue jean theme in "Between Blue Eyes and Jeans." Merle Haggard sang about how good a woman looked in "makeup and faded blue jeans." But it wasn't entirely the man's appreciate eye checking out those blue jeans in song, Terri Gibbs 1981 hit "Somebody's Knockin'" sang about a man in his blue jeans who just might be the devil himself.

Mel McDaniel recorded another country slant on blue jeans in 1984 with his recording of "Baby's Got Her Blue Jeans On." Country mega-star Garth Brooks brought denim into the current country scene when he sang, "A pickup truck is her limousine, and her favorite dress is her faded blue jeans." Country singer Ricky Van Shelton sings "Baby you're a dish in them cutoff blue jeans."

Dozens of artists have titled songs "Blue Jeans". A recent Google search turned up that title being used by Keith Urban, Silvertide, Marc Broussard, Blur, Morris Lane, Glen Glenn, Shocking Blue, and many others.

Hip-Hop artist Sir Mix-A-Lot is turned on by "the jeans she's wearin'" on "Baby's Got Back" and the Muckland Crooners are also looking to the denim rear when they recently recorded "Back Fat Blue Jeans" with the in-your-face hip-hop lyrics "Honey put your butt crack back in your blue jeans"

Whatever the motivation or reason, art, music, and literature have all been affected by the phenomenon of denim and throughout the years, artists, writers and musicians have incorporated the lowly blue jean into their art. Because they did, many of us find ourselves thoughtlessly humming some little tune with an innocuous lyric like "he wore black denim trousers and motorcycle boots...."

# Dealers and Collectors
## The '90s Yen for Old Denim

Prior to 1980, most worn-out American blue jeans became painting pants, went to the Salvation Army or Goodwill, were made into rags, or were simply thrown out. True enough, a minuscule amount of used jeans, primarily Levi 501s, were finding there way overseas and being sold at flea markets and second-hand shops and stalls. Despite the rumors and urban legends that told of a pair of jeans selling for $1,000 in Russia, not a lot of people were getting wealthy selling the discarded denims of America.

Old jeans were street fashion, or for cultists who were in love with things American. Germany, France, and England seemed to provide the biggest demand for used blues. If you wanted a pair of secondhand jeans in this country, almost any thrift store could oblige you for about a buck a pair. A lot of those were good jeans, almost new sometimes because American denim was so tough that many people outgrew their jeans before they wore them out.

In addition to that, with the ever-changing fickle buying habits of many Americans, there was a lot of denim out there that never sold. It got stored away in the basement or the warehouse while the next "hot" thing went on display. These items were known in the trade as "dead stock," inventory that, for one reason or another, couldn't sell. It seemed even the most diligent of merchants would always end up with some dead stock to dispose of. If it didn't get thrown out, it was stashed in stockrooms or basements, buried away for decades.

As the popularity of wearing and collecting vintage clothing grew in this country that new, but old stock, or "dead stock" began to see the light of day again. What came out with a lot of the dead stock was denim. Except for its novelty value, it wasn't worth much in those days. At least not to most Americans who would rather just buy a brand new pair of jeans. But there were some who looked at those old dusty piles of blue and saw green. Just as any other new product, all you had to do was fill a demand. If no demand existed, you could create one.

There are many who might take the credit for creating that demand, so they all will go nameless here. But a few young Japanese who were in tune to their peers back home, were busy rounding up the bits and pieces of American culture and sending them back to Japan.

Was it truly a fad, or a carefully-contrived plan by the few who had the supply? Very shrewdly, the supply was leaked out into the marketplace ever so slowly. With Americans going through millions of pairs of denims a year, to say nothing of what accumulated over the past half a century or so, it wouldn't pay to flood the market.

Even as these modern-day treasure hunters scavenged the back roads of America for more, Tokyo became the planetary Mecca for vintage denim buyers and sellers. An estimated 2,000 tons of vintage and contemporary denim found their way to Japan every year and still it wasn't enough for masses of eager Japanese youths. Rare vintage Levi 501s sold for thousands of dollars (not yen) with older jackets commanding even higher prices. There are subtle distinctions in these "old jeans," but those subtleties meant a big difference in value, price, and, of course, status.

To most Americans, a jean is a jean. A Levi 501 is a Levi 501. A Lee Storm Rider jacket is a Lee Storm Rider jacket. As long as they are not too worn out, we don't care if they were made in 1940 or 1990. They are, on the surface at least, the same jeans we grew up in; the same jeans our fathers wore.

To collectors, aficionados, and buyers and sellers of vintage denim. It is the subtle differences and the rarity of these old garments that makes one an old Buick and another a Dusenberg. They're both cars, but quite different. Values of taste, quality, rarity, cost, demand, and status were associated with each one. It is the

## Dealers and Collectors

same with most collectible objects. And they're are always different levels of collectors with varying levels of interest, passion for collecting, and knowledge about collecting, buying, and selling.

Earmarks of quality included the "Big E," the little red cloth tab Levi Strauss added to their 501 jean, and most other Levi pants, beginning in 1936. The little red tab sewn into the side seam of the right hand back pocket simply said "LEVI'S." Until 1971. The distinctions are subtle for those who are knowledgeable about vintage denim. All that changed in 1971 was the letter E, which became lower-case. However, "Big E" could add double to ten times the value on nearly identical garments.

As in most commodities, supply and demand establish value and rarity; and condition, as in almost any antique or collectible, would help to determine price. It is safe to say there are certain Japanese and some, though fewer Americans, who have made a great deal of money in buying and selling used denim; a few became millionaires. People noticed when word spread that a single Levi's denim jacket from the early 1940s sold for $5,000; that an earlier Lee jacket changed hands for $40,000, and that a pair of buckleback early 501s sold for $10,000.

The hunt was on, and people got to work trying to find similar treasures. In the antique world, these people are known as "pickers" and "scouts," the true hunters. For many, it is an everyday treasure hunt that leads them through the dusty garages, basements, and attics of people having garage or yard sales. A single pair of older "Big E" jeans could bring a picker hundreds or thousands of dollars. Some would stake out the local Salvation Army or Goodwill stores, waiting for the previous night's donations to be wheeled out on to the sales floor. Most newspapers carried ads by people willing to buy old denim. Around the country, small stores sprang up to buy and sell Levi 501s. In many small towns, especially in the West and mid-West, traveling buyers would set up shop for a few days, advertising locally to buy used denim.

A 1994 Esquire magazine article on denim said that at a Paris auction in 1992, a Levis promotional item from the 1930s, a pair of 501s on a cardboard cowboy, sold for about $75,000.

Accurate and authentic in almost every detail as their regular garments, jean manufacturers made these enormous pants to hang on store walls or to hang outside a storefront. Or, they made Lilliputian-sized pants as store giveaways to promote their particular brand of pants to customers. While still valuable, these more mass-produced items aren't as valuable as promotional items designed for in-store use. And as garments, unless you know some giants or six-inch tall midget buyers, these pieces aren't worth as much as their counterparts that were made at the same time but made in a wearable size.

**Responding to a foreign market for used denim, the signs went up and the search got underway in earnest. (and following pages)**

## 114 Dealers and Collectors

Dealers and Collectors 115

Vintage denim.

# Dealers and Collectors 117

True aficionados rediscovered the value in the original working blues.

## Dealers and Collectors

**Stores catering to the connoisseur cropped up in the hippest part of the coolest cities. (and following pages)**

## 120 Dealers and Collectors

# Dealers and Collectors    121

**James Dean beckons us back in time, to a jean depot at a flea market.**

## 124  Dealers and Collectors

**Denim dealers did a brisk trade at flea market venues.**

## Dealers and Collectors 125

Early morning Rose Bowl shoppers look over a stack of vintage denim in Pasadena, California.

Even cut-offs get a third lease on life in the brisk resale market.

## Evaluating Aged Denim

Size is just one of the many considerations when determining value of a vintage denim garment. For the most part, buyers of vintage denim want to buy merchandise that can be worn. Some items may be too rare and valuable to be worn, or their condition might be too fragile to withstand being worn, but even very old denim will be worn if it is wearable. Some collectors of vintage denim do buy just to collect, but the majority of vintage and used American denim is purchased to be worn. Buyers look for the following criteria in selecting denim to buy:

**Age:** How old is the garment? As in any collectible this is one of the primary criteria to determine value. The older the better, and the more valuable. Age can be determined by several style "clues" in most garments. In earlier denim garments, the way the denim was loomed differs from much of today's denim. Turn up the leg of a pair of Levi 501s for instance.

**Red lines:** Does it have a white strip, about a half-inch wide, visible on the inside of the seam? This is selvage, the edge of a woven fabric designed to keep it from unraveling. The white selvage is a giveaway to a pair of pants that most likely was loomed prior to the 1970s. Does it have a red thread on the inside of the seam? That "red-stripe" disappeared on 501s in 1986. These pre-1990s Levis have become the hot item as the really rare, older vintage denim has disappeared into collectors closets around the world. Known as "Red Lines" or "Akamimi" ( meaning "red ear") in Japanese, these pants can be readily identified from the outside by the black stitching at the top corners of the back pockets. Known to collectors and vintage hunters as "Black Flag," this stitching further identifies red lines that are worth almost twice as much on the market as are regular contemporary 501s. Red Lines are vintage, but not so old that they can't be found in large quantities.

**The "red flag" for vintage jean hunters.**

# Dealers and Collectors 129

**The white selvage is a giveaway to a pair of pants that most likely was loomed prior to the 1970s.**

**Seams and Selvages:** This particular kind of selvage also creates a slightly raised section of material along the outside seam. After several washings, this raised section, called "tracks" becomes obvious because it fades more quickly than the rest of the garment. It's called "tracks" or "tracking" because it resembles railroad tracks. For whatever reasons, used Levis with "tracking" are in high demand, especially in Thailand.

**Big Es:** Yet another way to determine age of a pair of Levi's. Big E or Capital E is an easy to find clues to age. We've already discussed the role of the Big E red tab on the side of the right back pocket of Levis and on the side of the left breast pocket on most Levi jackets. If the little red tab reads LeVI'S, it was most likely made after 1971. If the red tab bears a "Big E" in its LEVI'S logo, you are holding some real vintage denim manufactured somewhere between 1936 and 1971.

The selvage creates a slightly raised section of material along the outside seam called "tracks."

**Rivets:** Are there rivets? Where are the rivets? Are they on the back pockets? What are the rivets stamped with on the inside of the rivet? Experienced Levi's buyers can date some garments simply from what letter or numeral is stamped on the back of a rivet. Early Levis had rivets on the back pockets. These disappeared in 1936, supposedly in response to schools complaining to Levi Strauss that the copper rivets on the back of their jeans were tearing up chairs on school desks. Others say it was cowboys wearing Levi's complaining that the rivets were scarring up their leather saddles. If you see rivets on the back pockets of most denim jeans, chances are good, they pre-date 1937. Levi's jeans that came out after 1937 had hidden rivets. These "concealed rivets" as the company called them, were hidden on the inside of the pocket until double stitching replaced them in the early Sixties.

The copper crotch rivet that used to be on Levi 501s, Lee jeans, and other denim pants disappeared around World War II. There had been many complaints, but the banishment began in 1941 when Levi Strauss President Walter Haas Senior went camping and got himself, and the crotch of his Levi's, a little too close to the campfire. He retained a miniature brand between the legs, and the crotch rivet disappeared from Levi's, the other brands soon followed suit.

**The rivets on the back pockets of Levi's disappeared in 1936.**

**Levi's first version of its classic denim jacket featured a single breast pocket.**

**Rarity:** How rare is this garment? Were many made? Did many survive? This is tough information to come by, and it's not getting easier. Major manufacturers of denim, especially the Levi Strauss Co., are deluged with calls and letters from denim collectors seeking information. Due to the counterfeiting of many of their vintage garments and advertising, Levi Strauss is beginning to get very cautious with, if not downright suspicious of, vintage denim sellers and collectors. We appreciate their help, as well as that of Lee and Wrangler, and all denim manufacturers who contributed to this book.

**Condition:** What is the overall condition of the garment? Was it ever worn? Is it "Dead Stock" with the original labels or packaging intact? How worn is it? If it has been washed and faded, how even is the fading? How dark is the color? In today's markets, color or degree of fade has a lot to do with pricing. In the 1990s, Japanese buyers preferred deeper blue colors with less fade. Europeans, Greeks, Italians and others preferred a very faded, overall light blue look.

Was it dyed with real indigo dye? Older fabrics, especially like those used in 501 Big E jeans, keep a darker, more grainy blue color than contemporary jeans. It's most obvious if you put the two garments side by side to see the difference. Once you recognize the older, darker indigo, fabric, they will stand out on a rack of a hundred jeans. It's all a matter of education.

Does it have many holes? How big are the holes? Does it have any rips, tears, or open seams? Can it be sewn back together? Is there enough usable on the garment that it can be used for parts? (Yes, jean sellers do "part out" some vintage denim jackets to make another piece whole again) Are all of the buttons there? Is the original label still intact and legible? Has the garment been written on, painted on, had patches sewn on it? Is it repairable?

**Size:** What is a "good size", anyway? Average size is generally important when looking at vintage denim that will be sold to be worn. Denim buyers will generally only buy pants that meet certain waist and length (inseam) sizes.

**Brand:** Levi 501s are the gold standard for denim buyers. It is the most sought after and the most widely-purchased garment at both wholesale and retail levels.

## Jackets

Levi's denim jackets are the most consistently in demand, followed by Lee and Wrangler brand. Other brands come in behind that. In jackets, many of the same criteria apply for judging the value of a garment and its desirability as the requirements for pants. Other things to look for in jackets are whether it is lined or unlined and condition of the lining. Also, many newer jackets have side pockets that are not as desirable and generally mark the jacket as a contemporary garment. Check the labels carefully. Look for that Big E tab to help date a jacket. Generally, denim jackets with a single breast pocket and a buckle cinch in back are the earlier jackets and are worth more. Some of these early jackets are hanging on hangers in vintage shops sporting four and five digit price tags. Early Levi jackets date back to the 1920s. Labels might be marked with a style number ranging from 213 for some of the first jackets to 506XX for the 1938 model.

Generally, unlined jackets are worth more than lined jackets, Blanket lined jackets are worth more than fleece-lined jackets, which some dealers won't buy at all. Jackets with one breast pocket generally denote an older vintage jacket. Jackets with two breast pockets are worth more than those with four pockets (two breast pockets and two "hand-pockets" generally cut into the jacket and hidden on the inside). Off brand names, those not part of the "big three" of Lee, Levi, and Wrangler, are also collectible, but not as valuable. Denim jackets designed for use in prisons, or as railroad and work clothing, are generally much longer in length, hitting about mid-thigh, and usually have at least four pockets. They may be lined or unlined and again, the older, the more valuable.

White denim jackets, especially earlier models, are in demand, but not as valuable as blue denim. Other colored jackets have not as yet found any popularity with most collectors. Acid-washed, stone-washed, or bleached jackets, like pants that have been similarly treated, are also generally not collectible. Levi did make some "jean" jackets in leather and suede in the late 1960s and early 1970s. These jackets were cut using the same pattern as the Levi two-pocket, short-waisted jacket and usually sport a Big E tab. In its more than a hundred years of manufacturing, Levi Strauss has entered the marketplace with a wide variety of clothing styles and fabrics, as well as a myriad of other products labeled "Levis." These included laundry bags, placemats, notebooks, binders, shoes, and hats. They even had their name on a car when American Motors Jeep introduced one of their four-wheel drive vehicles outfitted with Levi's denim upholstery.

**Levi's are, as in pants, the gold standard in jacket collecting.**

**Dealers and Collectors 135**

**Five vintage Levi's jackets.**

## Dealers and Collectors

Dealers and Collectors 137

Near mint, vintage jackets.

## 140 Dealers and Collectors

# Dealers and Collectors 141

On the rack, a denim work jacket with corduroy collar.

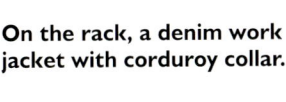

Japanese enthusiasts drove prices on the resale market during the 1990s.

# Postscript
## *The 21st Century and Ebay*

So what about now? What about Vintage Denim in the 21st Century? This book was originally written in the mid-nineties when the world itself and the world of vintage denim were a lot different.

The 21st Century now has the phenomenon of e-bay and other on-line global auctions serving as a marketplace for buying and selling anything and everything, including vintage denim. Now collectors, buyers, and sellers can sit at home and buy and sell and choose from thousands of items of vintage denim at almost any time.

For the purist, like it has been for most antique and collectible categories, the internet has taken a lot of the fun out of it. It is not the same thrill of the hunt, and the excitement of discovery when you find a true vintage denim relic amongst a rack of secondhand clothes. And often at very cheap price. That's what made it fun. Now, more peple then ever know about the "value" of vintage denim, and it is rare to find a bargain on the internet. Supply is up, demand is not as high, and prices have gone down.

What has that done to the value of truly vintage denim? In the early days of collecting vintage denim, the Japanese represented the vast part of the market for vintage garments, and their healthy economy created an amazingly healthy market for those garments. Prices were generally high, demand was high, and supply was low. Once Japan suffered some economic downturns, the value of most vintage denim plummeted severely. Extremely rare garments still held their value, but the run-of-the-mill denim prices sank to the value of secondhand clothing in many respects. For example, Big E Levi's jackets that once were selling for $500 to $1,000 were now only bringing $50-75.

Even though Americans finally acquired some taste and appreciation for vintage denim, the prices in this country never rivaled what they once reached in foreign markets. Today it is generally cheaper to find and buy vintage denim then it is to pay the prices commanded by the "new" Levi's that only look old, worn, dirty, wrinkled, and grungy. The desire for worn and comfortable jeans is still there, but it seems now very few want the "used" condition of vintage denim. They want things to "look old" but still be new. Used denim has found its way into the world of recycling and, perhaps someone's cherished old blue jeans are now the insulation in the walls of your new home!

The good news is there are still a lot of collectors and there is still good vintage denim waiting for you to discover. Whether you want to shop with the convenience of online markets or go out and dig through the thrift stores, garage sales, and flea markets of America, it's still there. Perhaps your find will lead to celebrity status when you show up on the Antiques Road Show with your buckle-back Levi's dating to the 1920s and worth thousands. It can still happen!

Money aside, a well worn pair of jeans provides a comforting connection with our past. Each pair is imbued with memories of holey knees, gooey, sticky ironed-on patches, big cuffs full of dirt and grass, the summer rite of cutting off last year's jeans, the trips to the store for new, dark-blue, stiff jeans to go back to school, sitting in the tub to shrink those new jeans tight, cutting them off to fray the cuffs, pegging them to get them "tapered" so tight we had to turn them inside out to get them off. We remember how good our jeans felt, and as we got older, how good someone else's jeans felt.

No matter where they came from, who wore them before, how much was paid for them, how rare they might be, how "in" or "out" of fashion they might be, our jeans will always be full of memories for us. And for everyone everywhere.

They will always remind us of softness, comfort, warmth, youth, and a sentimental connection to our past. Our jeans don't ask much of us, maybe a trip through the washer now and then, and they give us so much.

It's good to know that our "old jeans" have gained a reverence and an appreciation in the world of "vintage denim." Somehow it seems a sign of respect that our jeans should go on to a new life instead of becoming a painting rag.

An advertising slogan says "Cotton: The fabric of our lives" and those of us who wear cotton denim know that to be true. Our lives are woven into our jeans; a cotton canvas of blue memories that offers us a continuity of comfort, a link to our pasts and to one another, and most of all, a hearty "welcome" whenever we pull them on.